The 5 Senses

Text: **Núria Roca**

Illustrations: **Rosa M. Curto**

BARRON'S

If you try to taste this book, your parents are sure to tell you not to. It would be silly to lick a book! Fortunately, you have other **senses** besides your tongue to know what things are like. You have eyes to see, ears to listen, a nose to smell, and the skin all over your body to notice the touch and feel of things around you.

I see two things that are ... GREEN! They are white underneath, they have laces, they are empty inside—unless I get my feet in them! You know what they are, don't you? With your eyes you can **watch** lots of things, even some that are so far away you cannot touch them, such as the clouds floating in the sky.

You can **see** the color of things, their size, and you may even know if the things that surround you are moving or not. If they are not hidden, of course!

6

At night, we are so sleepy we can't keep our **eyes** open. Our eyelids feel heavier and heavier until finally we fall asleep. During the day, our eyelids move up and down all the time, cleaning our eyes, as if they were windshield wipers.

The sense of **sight** is so important that the eyes are protected by the eyelashes, which prevent dust getting in, and the eyebrows, which block the way of the drops of sweat!

The sense of **hearing** allows us … to hear! Sometimes, to hear a sound well, we have to pay attention. Shhhhh, listen! Can you hear how many sounds there are inside and outside your house? Some are so low it is hard to hear them, but others are so strong they may be heard from far away.

There are sharp **sounds,** such as the horn of a car, and also grave sounds, like the siren of a ship. I bet there are sounds you don't like in the least.

Close your eyes. I bet you have no problem in telling the direction from which a noise comes. That's how people who can't see play soccer: They attach a little bell to the ball so they may know **where it is.** The sense of hearing guides them!

Which sounds from the next page do you like best?

Do you know where the sense of **smell** is located? We can identify a thousand and one smells with it: Lemon, vinegar, cheese, peppermint, or cat's pee. Some smells are very nice and others are just horrible.

With your nose you may **"smell"** danger: If you smell something is burning, maybe it is the pie in the oven that is "in danger" of becoming a piece of charcoal!

When you have a cold, you can't smell well, can you? Your nose is so plugged up that you cannot notice the **smells** floating in the air or even breathe through the nose. It's a good thing we can also breathe through the mouth.

Your nose is running all the time, your eyes are all watery, and your tongue can't taste the flavor of things. You'd better wear warm clothes so you won't catch a cold.

Try to talk without moving your **tongue.**
You sound odd, don't you? The tongue is useful
for a lot of things: We use it to talk, to mix food in
the mouth, to stick out ... and to find out what
things **taste** like.
With the sense of taste you may tell the difference
between many different flavors.

The tip of the tongue notices if something is sweet or salty, the sides tell us when something is sour, and the back of the tongue notices when something is bitter. I bet you hadn't noticed that before, had you? Babies discover what things are like by putting everything in their mouths. Soon they learn whether the object is **tasty,** like marmalade, or **tasteless,** like a plastic toy. Which are your favorite flavors?

If you walk barefoot on the sand, you will notice the tiny grains that stick between your toes, feel if the sand is warm or cold, wet or dry. And you can experience it not only with your feet: **Touch** is a sense you have in the skin all over your body.

Have you ever noticed the tiny lines that cover the pad of your fingers? We call them fingerprints and they are different in every person. Your fingerprints are **unique** in the whole world!

Some parts of your body are so sensitive to touch that they **tickle** a lot, such as your armpits, your lips, or the palm of your hand. Try to tickle someone with a feather, and you'll see that they won't be able to resist without laughing for very long.

When your skin notices it is cold, the tiny body hairs stand up and you get "goose bumps," and when it notices it is hot, it sweats to refresh you. Your skin is very sensitive!

Cold, hot, dry, wet, soft, hard, straight, wrinkled, smooth, rough, or sharp: With your **skin** you may guess what many things around you are like, even without looking at them. Would you like to try?

Sometimes, some senses do not work properly or they don't work at all. This is the case with people who need glasses to see well, people who smell nothing, those who cannot hear any sound, or who cannot see anything at all. Can you feel with all of your **five** senses?

If one of your senses is not working properly, you will have to use the others better to know the world around you. If your hearing wasn't working well, which other sense do you think you would use more than now?

You feel your skin surrounded by warm water, you smell soap, you notice the bitter taste of shampoo, you hear the splash of water, and you see a shower. Where are you? In a bathtub, or anywhere else, your senses get along so well that they always work **together.**

And right now, what do you feel with your hearing, your sight, your taste, your smell, and your touch? Discovering the world through your five senses is a very challenging adventure.

Still Feet

A person tosses the ball in the air and says the name of one of the players. The player whose name is mentioned has to catch the ball and shout very loud "Still feet!"

Everybody stands still where they are and cannot move their feet or they lose and become "It." The player with the ball says the name of a player and tries to hit him or her with the ball.

If "It" hits the other player with the ball, the latter becomes the new "It," but if he or she dodges it or catches the ball with the hands, he or she will be "saved" and the first player will keep being "It."

Still

Your senses of sight and hearing will have to work extra hard!

The Blind Train

How is your sense of touch doing? If it is doing well, you may form a blind train with your friends. There may be as many players as you wish, from two to a hundred, and all you will need is handkerchiefs to make blindfolds. Form a line and hold the person in front by his or her shoulders. All the players must be blindfolded except the last one, who is allowed to see and will be the train engineer. This last player pats the shoulder of the player in front of him, who repeats the pat until it reaches the player who is in front. The pat may be on the right shoulder, the left shoulder, or the middle of the back and it means the player who is in the lead will have to go right, left, or straight ahead for five or six steps, and the rest of the train will follow in the same direction.

Be careful not to crash!

A Fish in the Fishbowl

Did you notice that sometimes our sight shows something we don't really see? You may confirm it by making a 3-inch square made of cardboard and a pencil with an eraser at the end.

1. Draw a fish in the middle of the square, as shown in this illustration.

2. On the other side of the square draw a fishbowl, right in the middle.

3. With a thumbtack, fix the square to the eraser at the end of the pencil. Hold the pencil with the palms of your hands and spin it back and forth. When the pencil is spinning very fast, you will see the fish is inside the fishbowl.

It's like magic!

1

2
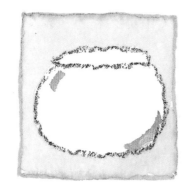

3

The Cow

You need one or more friends, blindfolds for your eyes, and a small bell or anything that makes noise when shaken. One of the players will wear the bell and will be the cow, while the other players, all blindfolded, try to tag the cow following the clinking of the bell.

The player who tags the cow takes over the role.

The Snail's House

This game is to test your sense of balance. Draw a snail like this on the ground, with fourteen squares and a house in the middle. The game consists of going through all the squares, hopping on one foot, starting in number 10 until you get HOME, where you are allowed to land on both feet and rest. Use one foot to go and the other to come back. The player who can go back and forth without failing wins the right to name one of the boxes, where he or she will be able to rest from now on. The other players will have to jump over the box with a name without stepping on it.

As the squares get named, the game gets tough!

Guidelines for Parents

Sight

Most people find more about the world with their eyes than with any other sense organ. Besides perceiving the color, the shape, and the size of objects, having two eyes allows us to perceive how thick and how far objects are. (Show the children how hard it is trying to catch a ball or playing hide and seek while keeping an eye closed. Explain that both eyes work together and when one of them is not working, it is hard to see where objects are.)

The eyes are protected by the eyelashes, which prevent dirt getting in the eyes; the eyebrows, which divert the drops of sweat or water that may slide down the forehead; and the eyelids, which open and close every two seconds without us even being aware of it. Eyelids clean the surface of the eyes and spread the lachrymal liquid that kills germs. Besides, when we are asleep, they cover the eyes to keep them moist and to prevent light and movement from bothering us.

Every year there are many people who suffer loss of sight due to accidents. We have to be very careful with games that require the use of sticks, toys that have sharp ends, or stones tossed into the air. It is important for children to see you wearing protection glasses when you do carpentry work or work in hobbies that may produce splinters. Education regarding work safety may begin in such an easy way as this.

A Very Different Taste

Taste is one of the senses that changes the most; that's why we like some food more or less depending on how hungry we are, the way it looks, or the texture it has. Besides, the way in which we perceive flavors changes as we grow older, because the amount of taste buds in our tongue diminishes with age. That's why some foods that are very tasty for adults have a flavor that is too intense for children. Thus, it is important to respect the sense of taste that children have, and to season their food accordingly. This does not mean depriving your children of the same food you eat: Their sense of taste must be trained by adding new flavors that they still find rather unappealing, although in small quantities.

Everybody usually ends up eating what they got used to at home. A good way to introduce new meals or to give children food they don't like very much is by way of a thoughtful presentation. Vegetables may look more appetizing if they are puréed; even spinach becomes more attractive when it is mixed in a lasagne. Sometimes success is achieved by cutting the food and displaying it on the dish in an appealing way.

A good way to educate the sense of taste is by allowing the younger members of the family to help during meal preparation. Not in vain, the sense of smell works closely with the sense of taste.

Hearing

The external part of the ear is called the pinna. The auditory meatus is a channel a bit over 1 inch in length that has hairs and earwax to catch dirt and other foreign matter. The meatus starts at the pinna and ends at the eardrum. The eardrum is a very thin membrane that vibrates when a sound reaches it as if it were a drum. At the end of the ear there are some tiny bones called malleus, stapes, and incus, which form a sort of bridge spanning the eardrum and an oval opening called the fenestra ovalis (another thin membrane, similar to the eardrum, that communicates with the inner ear). These three tiny bones, the smallest in our body, amplify the vibrations that reach the eardrum and send them to the inner ear, where sounds are received. Both ears work together to locate the sound. If one of them fails, sound perception is affected and it is hard to determine where a sound comes from. You may check it by covering one of your ears and trying to locate the sound of the alarm of a hidden clock.

Cleaning the ear is very simple, and should be limited only to the external ear. The channel should not be cleaned, and cotton swabs should not be used because they push the earwax further in. When blowing your nose, do not blow too hard, because the nose and the middle ear are connected by means of tiny holes and germs could get through.

The Sense of Balance

Keeping your balance, walking, and running demand some learning in which several senses must be synchronized. It is not until children are a little older that they reach a certain mastery of these skills. For example, until they are about four years old, children can't walk resting their weight on the heels or the toes alone. To improve the sense of balance and to make children aware later of the different parts of the body involved in each posture or movement, it is convenient to let them play games in which they have to jump, run, swim, ride a bicycle, ski, ride a scooter, dance, or do some acrobatics (always avoiding risks). This variety of movements,

that each child adapts to his or her own limitations and possibilities according to age, is indispensable to learn the motor coordination that ensures balance.

Touch

The sense of touch is spread over all the skin that covers our body, although some parts are more sensitive than others. Blind people can read thanks to the big amount of receptors found in fingertips. Their books are printed using a special code called Braille, a method in which numbers, punctuation symbols, and the letters of the alphabet are represented by characters made up of raised dots.

To take care of our skin we must keep it clean; however, we should not use soap in excess because that might destroy the skin's protective film. Allowing enough time for rest, massaging the skin, and keeping a balanced diet are good habits for our children's skin health as well as for other sense organs.

Teamwork

It is very seldom that one of the senses works completely alone, without the reference of any other one, because normally the five senses combine and are complementary. Thus, smell and taste cooperate to identify a certain flavor, just as sight and hearing work together to calculate and determine distance.

When one or more than one sense fails, the other senses overdevelop to compensate for the lack of information. For example, children who cannot hear well use sign language or lip reading to communicate, so sight works harder, while people who cannot see use the sense of touch, among others, to communicate. Try finding out with your children which senses are more common in different situations: cooking, studying, playing … the list you can make will be long.

First edition for the United States and Canada
(exclusive rights), and the rest of the world
(nonexclusive rights) published in 2006 by
Barron's Educational Series, Inc.

© Copyright Gemser Publications, S.L., 2006
C/Castell, 38; Teià (08329) Barcelona, Spain
(World Rights)
Tel: 93540 13 53
E-mail: info@mercedesros.com
Author: Núria Roca
Illustrator: Rosa M. Curto

Address all inquiries to:
Barron's Educational Series, Inc.
250 Wireless Boulevard
Hauppauge, NY 11788
http://www.barronseduc.com

ISBN: 978-0-7641-3312-1

Library of Congress Control Number: 2005931431

Manufactured by L. Rex Printing Company Limited, Dongguan, China
Date of Manufacture: August 2013
9 8